PRIME TIME
PREACHING

Planning Services on Sensitive Subjects

Eldon Weisheit

SAINT LOUIS

"In His Glory" reprinted from "A Time to Worship," *Youth Ministry Quarterly* (vol. 22, no. 4, Winter 1990). Permission granted from the LCMS Department of Youth Ministry.

The Scripture quotations in the choral reading, "In His Glory," are taken from the HOLY BIBLE, NEW INTERNATIONAL VERSION®. NIV®. Copyright 1973, 1978, 1984 by International Bible Society. Used by permission of Zondervan Publishing House. All rights reserved.

All other Scripture quotations from the Good News Bible, the Bible in TODAY'S ENGLISH VERSION. Copyright © American Bible Society, 1966, 1971, 1976. Used by permission.

Copyright © 1997 Concordia Publishing House
3558 S. Jefferson Avenue, St. Louis, MO 63118-3968
Manufactured in the United States of America

Library of Congress Cataloging-in-Publication Data

Weisheit, Eldon
    Prime-time preaching : planning services on sensitive subjects / Eldon Weisheit.
      p.   cm.
    ISBN 0-570-04977-6
    1. Sermons, American. 2. Worship programs. 3. Christian life—Lutheran authors. 4. Drama in public worship. 5. Christian drama, American. 6. Children's sermons.   I. Title.
BV4253.W4 1997
264'.041—dc21
                                       97-7487

1 2 3 4 5 6 7 8 9 10   06 05 04 03 02 01 00 99 98 97

Contents

Preface

When the editors at Concordia Publishing House asked me to write resource material for eight sermons on sensitive subjects, I was eager to get the list they had made. I liked the idea—and when their list arrived, I liked it too.

To check out the unknown committee who made the list, I asked a number of Bible classes and discussion groups, in the congregation I served and others, for their list of sensitive subjects. All the subjects on the list given to me also were suggested by someone in my survey. Many topics suggested from the survey are not treated in this book.

For example, there are no sermon suggestions on homosexuality, drug or alcohol addiction, child abuse, and many other topics. Many highly sensitive subjects are lumped together under the topic "Sanctity of Life." Other subjects that you would have included are also important—but this book is not offered as an encyclopedia of sensitive subjects. The ideas suggested here may help pastors deal with other issues that are important to them and their congregations. This short list may make others aware of the importance of helping people in many areas via the worship services of a Christian congregation.

Not only is the number of subjects limited but also the material about each subject. Just as a sermon has time limitations, so this book has space limitations. By the way, those limitations are a blessing, not a curse, because we are forced to get to the heart of the matter quickly—which is best for sensitive subjects. I am sure that I will be faulted for what I have not said on each of the eight subjects, just as those who preach on these subjects will not be able to say everything their hearers need. Aware of this, I have made suggestions for each preacher to supply additional applications according to local needs.

These worship suggestions are offered with a strong conviction that sermons can affect the lives of people and the life of a congregation. That conviction is based on my experience seeing the Holy Spirit at work through the Scriptures as they apply the Gospel of Christ to those who preach and those who listen.

Eldon Weisheit

Why So Sensitive?

This book offers suggestions for eight worship services that include sermons on what have been deemed sensitive subjects. These subjects are regarded as sensitive because they cover issues that are often difficult for people to discuss in families and over coffee at work. They also are sensitive because when they are discussed, the discussion often becomes an argument.

Sensitive subjects are even more difficult to present in a worship service because the response is either delayed until after the service or nonexistent. Yet if these important issues are covered only in Bible classes and private conversations, the great majority of the people in a congregation will not be exposed to them within the context of the church fellowship. Those who attend church may assume (properly?) that if a subject can't be mentioned in a sermon, then it should not be discussed elsewhere in church circles. On the other hand, if it can be mentioned in the worship service, the subject could be discussed in more detail later and in private.

The fact that these sermons are on sensitive subjects means that those who made the list, and the one who prepared the suggestions, do not think this material will resolve the issues discussed. Neither will your sermon. Those who preach do not solve the problems of those who hear their sermons. But sermons can help people know that both God and fellow Christians are aware of the concerns they have for themselves and their loved ones. A sermon can help people deal with their personal issues and can help those who hear the sermon help those who don't hear it. That's called equipping the saints.

Sometimes sermons on sensitive subjects do more harm than good because they only reinforce previously held opinions. For example, a stirring sermon on the evil of drunkenness (not one of our eight sensitive subjects) could have a number of results. It could make closet drinkers feel even more guilt and drive them from church. It could make those who live with problem drinkers feel even worse about their situation. And worst of all, it could make nondrinkers self-righteous and glad that "the preacher finally told drunks what they need to hear." Sensitive subjects are not handled well under the Law because that makes the guilty feel even more guilty, and it makes those who are sinners but don't have the particular temptation feel that they are better than others.

Therefore, do not preach sermons on sensitive subjects with a tone of authori-

ty or condemnation. That method will prove that the preacher is right (which may be true), but it will not help the sinner in the pew and the sinners who are afraid to occupy a pew.

Instead, preach sermons on sensitive subjects by asking questions and showing concern. The mirror of the Law asks, "Could this be you?" If it is, I'm glad you're here so you also can see yourself at the foot of Christ's cross. Sermons on sensitive subjects must see sinners not as criminals waiting for trial, but as spiritually ill people who need a doctor. We see our sins and the sins of others not as faults that must be condemned, but as problems that need help.

The purpose of these sermons is to help move these subjects from the court of justice to the throne of grace. The court of justice is needed, and as citizens of a country, we are concerned about the criminal part of any sin. We must deal with crime when we "give to Caesar the things that are Caesar's." That is part of our citizenship.

But as the church of Jesus Christ, we have something much greater to offer. When we give to Jesus that which is His, we can give something much greater than any law enforcement or judicial system has to offer. We move the subject to the throne of grace and offer the forgiveness and help that we have received from Christ to others who have the same needs—even if it is on different subjects.

Another reason that these subjects are difficult to treat in the worship service of a Christian church is that the solution is so obvious. These sensitive subjects are clearly right or clearly wrong. The objective is not to prove what is right or what is wrong. That has been done in God's Word. These sermons start from the point of knowing what is right and what is wrong rather than ending there. The purpose of the sermons is to change the hearts, the words, and the actions of those who worship. It is to help people in their needs. Then it is to help people help others in their needs.

Those of us who preach need to have our personal convictions on these sensitive subjects. That may become a problem if our conversations, reading material, and the speakers we hear at conferences have the same point of view as we have. Because we are influenced by those who agree with us, it is easy to think that those who don't agree are theologically, morally, and intellectually challenged. Our being right (which, indeed, we may be) makes it more difficult to communicate to those with different views.

A recommendation: Talk with people who have different views than yours on these and other sensitive subjects. The purpose of the conversation is not to prove your point but to understand why the other person has a different view. Read books and articles by people with a different view to see how they use the Scriptures, what their motives are, and how they reach their conclusions. Attend lectures, conferences, and discussions that present views contrary to yours. You need to know why these other views influence people, even members of your congregation.

In the situations suggested above, pay special attention to how the speakers or writers talk about people with different views. Do they

- use extreme examples of people who hold views similar to yours and imply, or even say, that all who hold your position are extremists?

- use degrading names and abusive language to describe people of your persuasion?

- state your position in a way that you would not agree with their version of it?

- accurately state what you believe and then tell others why you believe what you do—and be totally wrong about your motives?

- imply that those who think as you think are theologically, morally, and intellectually challenged?

Notice what happens if those with whom you disagree speak in some or all of the above ways. You defend yourself—aloud or in your mind. You see how wrong they are. They have reinforced those who already agree with them, but they have made you more sure you are right—and they are wrong.

Now imagine that people who don't agree with you hear your sermons on sensitive subjects. Will they think you have treated them in any of the ways suggested above? Will you reinforce their present views rather than change their thinking?

I had to learn how to speak on sensitive subjects and still preserve my integrity when I was a pastor in the deep South during the racial struggles. On Sundays I preached to people who had been taught racial prejudice by their families, schools, government, and in many cases, their churches. I also had opportunities to speak about racial prejudice to other groups that were strongly opposed to discrimination. I developed a way of speaking honestly without overstating my case. When speaking at home, I always pretended one of my civil rights worker friends was in a pew. When speaking in other places, I always pretended a member of the KKK was in the audience. I recommend the method to you as you speak on sensitive subjects.

One story from those days in the '60s needs to be shared because it helped me keep a balance, and it may do the same for you. While living in Mississippi, I was invited to speak at Yale Divinity School. (I called myself an exchange rabble-rouser.) During one question and answer period, a divinity student kept referring to "Southern White Males" in a tone of voice that clearly showed that he didn't like them. I finally asked him how many Southern white males he knew. His answer? "None. But I know what they are like." And I was there to oppose prejudice!

Questions will change people more than sharing your personal conclusions. Compassion will change people more than judgment. Check the gospels to see how Jesus helped the people who wanted to argue with Him about theological and moral issues. He asked questions, and He told stories.

One more suggestion for preaching sermons on sensitive subjects. Do a voice check with someone outside your family. These subjects arouse emotions. Our voices and body language reflect those emotions. Often we want to sound confident; instead, we sound angry. Often we want to sound sincere; instead, we sound bored. Check it out.

A few suggestions on ways that a parish pastor might use the resources in this book.

- The sermons could be a series, using all or a selected number of the sermons. If you want to use all of them, it might be better to do two series of four each. Publicize the series by mentioning the subjects. Frame the invitation to emphasize that the series is not just for people dealing with the issues under discussion (most people won't admit they are affected by some of these issues) but also for those who want to give Christian help to those who have such needs.

- The sermons and other suggested resources may be used one at a time as needed or when they fit into other liturgical or program schedules. Again, announce the sermon as a way of helping church members help others.

- The material offered can be a resource for preaching on other texts that deal with these subjects and used as part of the regular preaching schedule of a congregation.

- The material could be used for discussion groups and/or Bible classes. There is a great advantage in presenting sensitive subjects in a situation where people can respond to the presenter and to one another. However, this method probably will reach fewer people, and some who have special needs may not feel comfortable coming to a session dealing only with the topic that affects them.

2

Prejudice

Why So Sensitive?

Prejudice is a difficult subject for the church because it is a matter of the heart and mind. The laws of the nation must deal with the *actions* of its citizens—not their *thoughts.* So in the court of justice, prejudice can work underground to give energy to individuals and to groups to commit acts of violence, injustice, and greed. Those who spoke out against racial prejudice in our country in the '60s and '70s, and those who gave their lives fighting such prejudice, had to be content with passing laws that affected the results of prejudice. But the roots of such crimes are still intact in the hearts of people.

Racial discrimination was only one of many manifestations of the root of prejudice. That struggle opened the eyes of many to see other prejudice based on gender, age, disability, religion, regionalism, and more. Those who recognize prejudice as the sin that leads to many of society's crimes cannot rely on the courts to fight crime and lead the way in the fight against the evil of prejudice. It is the church that must move the issue to the throne of grace.

To many, prejudice is not a sin. Some even see it as a virtue. It often is difficult to bring prejudice under the condemning message of God's Law because individuals and groups see only the prejudice in other individuals and groups, not in themselves. The evil of prejudice can cover itself in a cloak of self-righteousness because we feel that by condemning the wrongs of others we somehow make ourselves right. Those who oppose the evil of prejudice may in the end become prejudiced against the people they oppose.

Also, the church often finds itself handicapped in identifying prejudice as a sin because we often promote religious prejudice. In the name of standing for moral and theological truths, we may cause prejudice against others rather than repentance and change. To help people in the struggle against prejudice, we must not only show them the sin that it is and the sin that it causes, but we also must show them the throne of grace that offers forgiveness to those who are prejudiced against sinners.

Prayer of the Day

Lord Jesus, open our eyes to see people as You see them and open our hearts to love people as You love them. Amen.

Sermon

Text: James 2:1–9

Concept: Check Your People Vision

The text for today's sermon is an eye test. This test does not measure if you are nearsighted or farsighted. It does not look for cataracts in your eyes. Rather, the test is to see how you look at people.

I ask you to look around at the people worshiping with you today. What do you notice about these people? Now think of the people you see in your daily lives—the ones you know and the strangers you encounter every day. What do you see? Now think of the people you see on TV and read about in papers, magazines, and books. What do you think about those people?

I have a number of eyeglasses here. I invite you to try them on with me to see how we see one another and how we see people in the world around us. Each set of glasses is a prescription ground into the lenses that affects the way we see people.

Application: *(Use in any order according to your congregation's needs. Add others according to local need.)*

1. The lenses in this pair have dollar signs ground into the glass. Some of the people to whom James wrote the words of the text wore these glasses. When you wear these glasses, you see people according to their financial worth. These lenses make the people who are rich look like good, important people. They make poor people look bad and unimportant. *(Discuss the admonition of the text about judging people by financial status.)* Do you own a pair of glasses with this kind of lenses?

2. The second kind of glasses comes with a number of tints. Some are tinted white, others black, red, yellow, or brown. These glasses are worn by those who are racially prejudiced. When we wear them, they make all people of a given race look exactly alike. People who wear these glasses think that all people of one color are good and all people of another color are not good. They measure morality, intelligence, and personal value by the color of skin. These glasses do not help us see

people as they really are. Instead, these glasses blind us from seeing that all people are our brothers and sisters—brothers and sisters because they were created by the same Father and redeemed by the same Savior. These colored lenses keep us from receiving the gifts that God has given to people of another skin color, and they prevent us from experiencing the joy of sharing our lives with them.

3. There are many other glasses that have the sin of prejudice ground into their lenses:

- Do you see people as good or bad according to age? Are all young people potheads or gang members in your eyes? Are all old people boring and bossy in your eyes?

- Do you see people by their occupation? Do you wear glasses that affect your vision of lawyers, members of the media, politicians, law enforcement officers, church leaders, telemarketers, and the like? Do the "bad ones" make you think that all are bad? Do the "good ones" make you think that all are good?

- Do you know what your prejudices are? Do you know where these prejudices came from? *(Tell a personal story about prejudice. You may substitute your own or use this story based on my experience as a pastor in the deep South in the late '60s.)* During the racial conflicts in Alabama, I preached a sermon in which I listed the Klu Klux Klan as one example of collective sin against God. Someone said, "You also should have named the Communists." I replied, "No one in this congregation is a Communist, and I don't think any are tempted to become one. But some might be members of the KKK and more might be tempted to join. My job is to talk about *our* sins, not someone else's." *(This sermon is not to help congregation members know how bad other prejudiced people are. It is to help them see their personal prejudices and to repent. Use other "glasses" as needed to help people see their prejudice.)*

4. We have one more pair of glasses to try on. This pair has a cross ground into each lens. These are the glasses that God wears when He looks at us through the eyes of Jesus Christ. Notice something very important about these glasses. They do not blind Him to the reality of sin. They are not rose-colored glasses that make the world look perfect. The message of the Gospel is that God has seen our sin and He has done something about it. He did not condemn our sin, He forgave it (John 3:17). He sent His Son, Jesus Christ, who paid the price of our sin. Therefore, when God looks at us through these cross-ground glasses, He sees the sins removed.

Through our faith in Jesus Christ, the prescription for looking at people through Christ has been ground into the glasses that we wear. We can see others through Christ's glasses. When we do, we do not ignore the wrong they have done. Some poor people may have spent their money on drugs or gambling. Some rich people may have cheated to get their money. Some people in racial minorities may be lazy or dishonest. Some people in racial majorities may be power hungry or unjust. Every prejudice may be based on a stereotype that has individual cases where it is true. But the sin of one does not mean all similar people have the same sin. Those who do sin need repentance and forgiveness. Those who wear Gospel glasses can offer that repentance and forgiveness.

But Gospel glasses do even more. A lot of prejudice is not based on real wrongs of individuals or groups. We often are prejudiced against others only because they are different—and we don't understand them. We don't forgive people for being rich or poor, black or white, young or old, or any other difference that causes classic prejudice. Instead, we should accept them as Christ has accepted us. The glasses that Jesus wears help us see other people as the created and redeemed children of God.

Conclusion:

This text asks you to do two things:

- Identify the glasses that you wear that make you prejudiced against individuals or groups.

- Wear the Gospel glasses that Jesus has given you by His death and resurrection. See others as Jesus sees them. Give your Gospel glasses to others. There always will be another pair for you.

Children's Sermon

Text: Luke 6:38c

Concept: A New Measuring Stick

Jesus says, "The measure you use for others is the one that God will use for you." Let's think about how we measure things. See this? *(Show foot ruler.)* This is a foot ruler. It's 12 inches long. Suppose I wanted to make one of you think you are tall. I could call this a yardstick, which is 36 inches long. *(Measure a short child.)* If this were a yardstick, you would be *(read ruler)* _____ feet tall. That isn't right. This is a yardstick. *(Show yardstick.)* You are really *(read yardstick)* _____ feet tall.

But Jesus is telling us something more important than how to measure height. He knows that we measure one another by the way we judge one another and the way we judge ourselves. Sometimes we want to make other people look bad by saying bad things about them. We sometimes make our own measuring stick—like saying this is three feet long when it is only one. We say other people have to do things that we do. Sometimes we think that others are wrong because they don't agree with us. We measure them by our way of doing things.

Jesus says that if we measure other people our own way, He will measure us the same way. If we tell everyone else they are bad, we are really saying that we are bad. He tells us this because we aren't the ones who decide what is good and what is bad. God did that when He gave us the Ten Commandments. God's rules are like this. (Hold up yardstick.) It is the right measurement. If we use God's measuring stick, we also have a problem because we cannot do everything that God tells us to do. If we use His commandments to show other people how bad they are, He will use those commandments to show us how bad we are.

But Jesus has another way of measuring us. Look at this. (Hold ruler and yardstick to form a cross.) This is how Jesus measures us. He obeyed all the commandments for us. Then He also paid for our sin when He died on the cross. When Jesus made the measuring stick into a cross, He changed the way God measures us. He gives us His love and grace. He sees us as His friends.

We also can use the measuring stick that Jesus uses. We can measure people by the love that Jesus has for them rather than by what we think of them. The yardstick is sometimes seen as a reminder of the punishment we deserve. But the cross shows us the love that God has for us.

For the Bulletin

1. When have you been the victim of prejudice from others?

2. Did your response add to or take away from the prejudice?

3. Do you recognize prejudice in yourself?

4. Where does it come from?

5. What can you do about your prejudice?

6. What specific people or situations make you need to wear Gospel glasses?

7. To whom would you like to give Gospel glasses before they look at you?

Through the Week

1. Watch the local, national, and international news as you check yourself for prejudice. Did any news event stir up anger and prejudice in you?

2. Check how other people express their prejudice. Do they expect you to agree with them? Do they think they have your approval?

3. Can you help remove prejudice in your family or workplace by seeing the situation through your Gospel glasses?

3

Violence

Why So Sensitive?

The church is a place of sanctuary—a place of peace in a world of violence. People who come to church do not want to hear about violence. They want to escape from it. That's one view. But another view says that unless we speak about the violence of the world to the people who come to church, we cannot give them the peace that Christ has earned for us to take back to a world that needs that peace. The question is: Is the church a place to escape from reality or a place to confront reality with the Gospel of Christ and change the world?

Violence is a reality of life. God's grace and peace through Jesus Christ are realities of life for those who believe in Him. It is the privilege of the church to bring these two realities together because we have the promise, "Don't think that there is no truth in the scripture that says, 'The spirit that God placed in us is filled with fierce desires.' But the grace that God gives is even stronger" (James 4:5–6).

We deplore the violence in nations who fight against each other or turn against themselves in civil wars. We are alarmed at the violence of gangs, the bombing of buildings and planes, the wild person on a roof with a gun, and militia who take the law into their own hands. Those things seem far away from most people in the pew. But violence is found also in the homes and the hearts of those who worship. Child- and spouse-abuse have reached near epidemic proportions in the United States. In this country, more than 15,000 people were killed by guns in 1994 (the last year with available statistics). The United States has about four-and-a-half times the population of England—a country that reports only 75 people killed by guns in 1994. If 15,000 U.S. citizens were killed in one crash or explosion, the event would attract the attention of the world. But when they are killed one or two at a time, their deaths go almost unnoticed. Families and neighbors often know that children or women are being physically or sexually abused, but they can't—or won't—do anything about it.

Violence will not be stopped by laws that start with the problem and work backward to the source. But violence can be reduced if we start at the source and eliminate the pressure that leads to violent acts. The church can move problem violence from the court of justice to the throne of grace.

> ## Suggested Readings
> **Psalm:** Psalm 35:1–9
> **First Reading:** Exodus 21:12–27
> **Second Reading:** James 4:1–9
> **Gospel:** Matthew 15:17–20

Prayer of the Day

Holy Spirit, remove the anger, frustration, and turmoil from our hearts by filling us with the love and peace that comes from Jesus Christ. Then send us back to our homes and work to share this love and peace with others. Amen.

Sermon

Text: James 4:1–9

Concept: Violence from the Heart

(Hold up uninflated balloon.) View this balloon as a nation, a community, a church, or as yourself. Something happens that causes anger. *(Blow one puff of air into balloon. Suggestion for smokers and other oxygen-challenged preachers: Inflate the balloon several times before using it in the sermon.)* There is conflict and disagreement. *(Blow another puff into balloon.)* There is competition and failure. *(Blow another puff into balloon.)* There is jealousy and fault-finding. *(Blow another puff into balloon.)*

You see what is happening. These feelings that cause insecurity and frustration and create a need for revenge are being stored up in a nation, a community, a church, or in you. They build up, sometimes very fast and at other times slowly over many years. Then one more event happens. Many times it is not as important or as tragic as the events already stored up, but violence occurs. *(Pop balloon with pin.)* War breaks out in a country. A community has riots, looting, and deaths. A church is divided and sometimes destroyed. What happens to you?

The text asks, "Where do all the fights and quarrels among you come from?" We're going to look for the answer from this text, from the words Jesus spoke in the Gospel that was read, and from our lives.

Application: *(Use in any order according to your congregation's needs. Add others according to local need.)*

1. Violence is the result of sin stored in an individual or a community. *(Use sermon text and Gospel reading to show how sinful emotions build up to cause fighting and quarrels.)* An empty balloon does not explode when pricked by a pin. A person who is not already filled with anger and the other items listed can handle daily frustrations and disappointments. One purpose of this sermon is to ask each of you: How close are you to exploding? Do you con-

trol your anger at work and in your social life but then burst into violence at home against family or alone against yourself?

2. Don't hide anger and other emotions that lead to violence. They become more destructive when they are denied. If you say you don't have a problem, you won't deal with the problem. The Bible is filled with violence. Some have criticized it and have said that children should not read certain stories. Some say that God Himself is part of the problem because He orders His people to do acts of violence.

The Bible deals with violence because it deals with people. Our sin and the sin of others cause the destruction we see in people individually and collectively. The Bible often speaks about violence because it happens often. That helps us know that God can help us on the subject. God has to face the issues caused by violence because He is our God and He is with us. In the Old Testament, God had a bad reputation among some because of the violence of His people. The people did the evil, and God is blamed. In the New Testament, Jesus suffered violence and death because He loved sinners. We did the wrong, and He took the blame.

3. The time to deal with violence is not when the balloon is ready to burst. Rather, the best way is to avoid the buildup of the things that lead to violence. For every person who becomes so filled with hate that he takes an uzi and heads to a rooftop or a bomb and heads for a public building, there are many others who are building up to that moment. For every person who is so filled with rage that he beats and kills a child or a spouse, there are many others who could reach that point of explosion. For every person who carries a gun and explodes in a parking lot or during a family quarrel, there are many others who left the gun at home or did not have a gun.

The number of people who commit violent acts is frightening, but even more frightening are the numbers that might do it. Be aware of the pressure building up in yourself. Do not let it reach the point where you will explode. Be aware of the pressure building up in members of your family and others around you. Do not add to that pressure.

4. The buildup of the emotions that lead to violence is part of the human condition, but it does not mean that violent acts are inevitable. The balloon that is at the breaking point need not explode. The pressure can be released slowly. We can change the question of the text to, "Where will all the fights and quarrels among you go?" When we take to Christ those things that cause the pressure that leads to violence, He eases the pressure. He forgives our sins so we need not defend ourselves and blame others. He forgives others so we need not carry the need for revenge. He takes the pressure off the person or the community that is in danger of violence. We protect ourselves from the violence of others not by attacking others and increasing the possibility of an explosion,

but by lowering our emotional level so we can deal with our struggles and then offer help to others.

5. There are some practical things for us to do. Know what blows up your balloon. Avoid subjects that fill you with anger. Sometimes your prayer, "Lead me not into temptation," must be answered by separating yourself from certain people, certain situations at work or in the family. You may have to quit watching certain TV programs or listening to talk radio.

Instead, you need to leave the people and situations and deflate the balloon that leads to violence. Our worship services are designed to lower hostility. Confess your sins and receive forgiveness. The pressure goes down. Recognize that all others are forgiven by Christ too. The pressure goes down. Give attention to the joy of worship and praise of God. The pressure goes down. Receive the body and blood of Christ with the joy of being with Him. The pressure goes down.

Now give to others what you have received. Know which subjects to avoid with certain people. Recognize that you might help some people by staying out of their way. "Goodness is the harvest that is produced from the seeds the peacemakers plant in peace" *(James 3:18, the words that immediately precede the text.)*

Conclusion:

It would help if each of us had a balloon over our head to show how near we are to an explosion. But we don't. You can, however, let other people know when you feel the pressure that leads to an explosion. You can ask for help. And you can recognize when others are near that point. You can help ease the pressure. Instead of an explosion of violence, there can be the joy of peace.

Children's Sermon

Text: 1 Peter 2:1–2

Concept: Who Gets to Name You?

(If practical, use a newborn baby from the congregation. Ask the baby's name. Ask children what they would name the baby. If no baby is available, talk about who named the children present.) Who gets to name the baby? *(Let children respond.)*

Other people have other names for us. *(Talk about names grandparents, teachers, and others may use.)* God calls us His friends. He says we are His children—even the adults are His children.

Sometimes people call one another bad names. *(Ask about things that happen in families or at school.)* We often hear children call one another bad names. The text tells us not to use bad words to insult others. Let's help ourselves in two ways.

First, no one else has a right to give you a bad name. Your parents named you. God has named you. When other people call you bad names, you don't have to feel bad about yourself. They have no right to give you a bad name. Don't accept the name. You know who you are because you have been named by people who love you. You are called a Christian because Jesus is your Savior. When you know Jesus is with you, you don't have to feel bad if someone else calls you a bad name.

Next, you cannot give bad names to other people either. If you call another person a bad name, you are hurting that person. Jesus loves that other person too. He has called that person His friend. You can help people by calling them good names. Then other people can call you good names too.

For the Bulletin

1. What or who makes you become like a balloon ready to explode?

2. What or who helps you release the pressure that builds up within you?

3. Do you know people who are ready to explode? What could you do to help them?

4. Make a prayer list of people who need relief from the pressures that could lead to violence.

Through the Week

1. Suggest ways for family members to see when another person is ready to explode. (One way might be for each person to draw a balloon that shows how much frustration they have inside. Then draw another balloon for each family member that shows how much anger they are showing to others.)

2. Make a list of things that add to the pressures of your life.

3. Make a list of things that decrease the pressures of your life.

Chancel Drama

(Place the following information [up to Director's Notes] in the bulletin.)

The Things That Come Out of the Mouth

Setting: A neighborhood cafe

Cast: Two adults who live and work in the community; waiter; waiter's friend; Holy Spirit (an unseen cast member in scenes 3 and 4)

Scene 1: Coffee break in the cafe

Scene 2: The next morning

Scene 3: Coffee break in the cafe

Scene 4: The next morning

> [Jesus said,] "But the things that come out of the mouth come from the heart, and these are the things that make a person ritually unclean. For from his heart come the evil ideas which lead him to kill, commit adultery, and do other immoral things; to rob, lie, and slander others." *(Matthew 15:18–19)*

Director's Notes

Setting: Two tables in small neighborhood cafe—checkered tablecloth, menu, sugar, salt, etc. Two chairs at each table.

Cast

Adult 1 (middle-aged man or woman)

Waiter (teenaged boy or girl)

Adult 2 (middle-aged man or woman)

Friend (teenaged boy or girl)

Scene 1

(WAITER is onstage. ADULTS 1 and 2 enter and sit at table.)

ADULT 1: *(to WAITER)* The usual.

WAITER: Two coffees—one black, one with cream.

ADULT 1: That really ticks me off.

ADULT 2: You mean the parking lot out there?

ADULT 1: Yes. I can't understand why we allow kids to destroy everything like that.

(WAITER enters with cups, serves ADULTS 1 and 2, and stands and listens to conversation.)

ADULT 2: They threw all the garbage out of the Dumpster. There's no sense in that.

ADULT 1: And those lawn chairs. The wind didn't blow them out of the neighbors' yards and deposit them in the parking lot. They stole those chairs.

ADULT 2: I hope the cops get them and give them a hard time.

ADULT 1: You know what will happen if they are arrested. Someone will talk about how sad it is that the kids come from broken homes or that both parents work. It will end up being our fault, as usual.

ADULT 2: They need more than a good talking to. Someone should take them out in that parking lot and give them a swift kick to the backside.

ADULT 1: Maybe someone should throw them in the Dumpster and turn it over so they couldn't get out.

ADULT 2: It would save the community a lot of problems and money if someone just shot them. Hey, it's time for me to get to work.

ADULT 1: We've already solved the problem with those dumb jerks. Let's see what we can do for the boss.

(ADULTS 1 and 2 exit as FRIEND enters and sits.)

WAITER: Hi! Want a Coke?

FRIEND: No bucks—no Coke! Just came by to see you. What happened to your parking lot?

WAITER: Someone messed it up. The good people in the neighborhood are getting tired of it.

FRIEND: Well, so am I. Does that make me one of the good people around here?

WAITER: They said someone should rough up the kids who did it—maybe even kill them.

FRIEND: That's the cops' job.

WAITER: They've got more important things to do than to care about us.

FRIEND: Maybe you're right. I think I know who did it.

WAITER: You ought to do something about it.

FRIEND: I'll talk to some of the guys after school.

Scene 2

(ADULTS 1 and 2 enter, talking as they sit down. WAITER brings coffee.)

ADULT 1: Did you hear the morning news?

ADULT 2: You mean about the two kids that the night security guy found in the Dumpster?

ADULT 1: Yeah, I guess they're in bad shape. One has a broken jaw, and the other kid may have a concussion.

ADULT 2: I don't know where all this violence comes from. It's bad enough for them to mess up property, but when they start hurting one another —that's awful.

ADULT 1: Parents just don't know how to raise kids anymore.

ADULT 2: I think it's the school's fault too, and the church's. Someone has got to do something.

Scene 3

(ADULTS 1 and 2 enter and sit at table.)

ADULT 1: What a mess!

ADULT 2: You mean the parking lot out there?

(WAITER enters with cups, serves ADULTS 1 and 2,
and stands and listens to conversation.)

ADULT 1: Yeah, someone really trashed the place. That worries me.

ADULT 2: And it looks like they carried off some lawn furniture too.

ADULT 1: What would you have done if you had seen them doing it?

ADULT 2: I'd have called the cops.

ADULT 1: Suppose the cops arrested whoever did it and then you had a chance to talk to them. What would you say?

ADULT 2: That's a tough one. I'd be angry at them, but I know it wouldn't do any good to yell. What would you say?

ADULT 1: I'm a Christian. I suppose I should tell them Jesus loves them and forgives them. I doubt that they'd be in a mood for that.

ADULT 2: But you could tell them that sometimes people who get into trouble with the law have to do community service. You could say that they could work for our church and we would supervise them if they cleaned up the neighborhood.

ADULT 1: I wonder if they'd listen if we offered to work out a swap with them. They help us keep the neighborhood clean and we'll let them play on the church's basketball court. Maybe we could even get a team from church to take them on in a game.

ADULT 2: Sounds good, but we're dreaming.

ADULT 1: What do you mean?

ADULT 2: Kids aren't going to listen to us. They'd think we're old and out of touch with reality, I mean like in space, you know, like wow!

(ADULTS 1 and 2 exit as FRIEND enters and sits.)

WAITER: Hi! Want a Coke?

FRIEND: No bucks—no Coke! What happened to your parking lot?

WAITER: Someone trashed it. I tried to call the boss to get someone to clean it up, but he's out of town. I don't know who will do it.

FRIEND: Do you know who did it?

WAITER: I don't have a clue.

FRIEND: If you did, what would you do?

WAITER: First, I've already called the cops. I guess I'd tell them.

FRIEND: What good does that do?

WAITER: Whoever did it has to be stopped or they will do even worse things. Maybe the cops would make them clean up this place—and even more—so they'd learn a lesson.

FRIEND: What if the people who did it cleaned up the place on their own.

WAITER: That'd be great.

FRIEND: If we knew who they were, how could we get them to do it?

WAITER: I've heard that the church on the corner would let kids from the neighborhood play on their basketball court. We might work out a deal with the church and whoever messed things up.

FRIEND: Let me talk to some of the guys at school. I'll get back to you.

Scene 4

*(ADULTS 1 and 2 enter, talking as they sit down.
WAITER brings coffee.)*

ADULT 1: I had a meeting at church last night and the strangest thing happened.

ADULT2 : What was that?

ADULT 1: A bunch of kids showed up with trash bags. They were cleaning up around church. I asked what was going on, and the youth director said the kids had cleaned up the mess in the parking lot here and then come over to the church to offer a deal. They said they'd clean up around there too, if they could play basketball. They're going to do it every Thursday evening.

ADULT 2: Isn't that strange. That's what we talked about.

ADULT 1: I know. But we didn't do anything. We just talked.

ADULT 2: Then let's do something. Let's play basketball next Thursday night—or at least cheer for the visitors.

(ADULTS 1 and 2 exit.)

(Un)Employment

Why So Sensitive?

In your mind look at the people who will be sitting in the pews when you preach.

- How many are unemployed and looking for work?

- How many are worried that they will lose their job in the near future?

- How many dislike their present job but think they must keep it because they need that paycheck and the perks that go with it?

- How many feel that their job violates their moral standards, but they must keep on working because of family responsibilities?

- How many feel inadequate to do the work required of them?

- How many feel underemployed and know they could handle a more responsible job?

- How many want to go back to school to qualify for another job but can't take time off without an income?

- How many are in school now and worry about finding a job after graduation?

Now look down those same pews again and see how many people sitting there are worried about a family member who has employment concerns as expressed in the questions above.

Even as you have identified the vocational problems for some members of your congregation, realize that many others have job-related stress that you are not aware of. Maybe they are too embarrassed to talk about their problems. Maybe it has not occurred to them that the problem is part of their spiritual life.

Now ask yourself the above questions. Those who work for the church also experience vocational restlessness. Think about places where you have worked previously. Are you concerned about the employment—present or future—of your family members?

One more question: Should those who have jobs that they enjoy—and in which they find fulfillment—be concerned about others in their Christian family who are worried about employment?

Employment is a sensitive subject because we often measure ourselves and others by paychecks and job titles. Those who have job security and good salaries may look down on those who don't, considering them lazy or inadequate. "We've got it made. What's wrong with them?"

Those who struggle with their jobs may feel like failures. Many people formed their opinions about careers long ago and do not realize that the rules have changed. They may take out the frustrations of the job on their families and others. Often they can't talk about their real problem because they think others won't understand. A church member once said to me, "When I lost my job, I felt I couldn't go to church because I couldn't give an offering. I was afraid someone would ask me to do something around church or something social that would cost money." The prophet Joel spoke for people during a famine who were troubled not only because they had no food for their families but because they had no offering to give God (Joel 1:13).

Those who come to worship should not have to check their worries at the door as they enter the church. Worship is not an escape from reality. Rather, it is a place to face difficulties in the presence of God and of brothers and sisters in Jesus Christ. They need help in applying the activity of worship to their reality. They need to leave church with an awareness that others understand their problem and that they have the support of a Christian community.

People who are anxious about their work are sensitive to anything that seems like pity or criticism. The church needs to be sensitive to their needs.

Suggested Readings

Psalm: Psalm 31:1–5
First Lesson: Genesis 1:26–30; 3:15–19
Second Lesson: 1 Peter 4:10–11
Gospel: Mark 6:43–45

Prayer of the Day

Lord God, as we are together now in the name of Jesus Christ, we also ask that our Savior will go with us this week to our homes and to our places of employment and study. Amen.

Sermon

Concept: From Home to Work—And Back Again

This sermon is written in digest form rather than an outline. Please don't read it to anyone but yourself because it is preached to you. After you have applied it to yourself, rework it according to the needs of the people in your church pews. Also please do not divide it into a series of three sermons, though each part could have enough material for a feature presentation. To achieve the purpose, all three parts must be offered to the same people at the same time.

Introduction

Two easy questions will help you understand how you feel about your life. They are: How do you feel when you go from home to work? How do you feel when you go from work to home? Some of you will substitute school for work, but use the same questions. Some of you who work at home, or have other work responsibilities that do not get a paycheck, can easily adjust the questions to fit your situation. How do you feel about the activities you do at home? How do you feel about the things you do to keep yourself busy? It's your life. Is it worthwhile?

We are going to look at three sections of Scripture to help you evaluate your life.

Part 1

Text: Genesis 1:26–30

God identifies Himself first as Creator. If we were to identify the gods that people worship and list them in the Yellow Pages, the God of the Jews and Christians would be listed first under *Creator.* We Christians know that we have something special because Jesus Christ is the only one in the gods' Yellow Pages under *Redeemer;* therefore, we sometimes forget the uniqueness of knowing God as our Creator. *(I usually do not feel a need for footnotes for studies such as this. However, I encourage the preacher to read* The Creators *by Daniel J. Boorstin, Random House, 1992, especially Part Two, "A Creator God," Chapter 5, "The Intimate God of Moses.")*

Knowing God as our Creator gives us a relationship with Him that also gives us a great responsibility. Check the text: We have the privilege of not only being created by God but of being part of His system of continuing creation. We have a collective responsibility to "have many children." There's the family. That doesn't mean all of us will become fathers or mothers, but it does mean that all of us are involved in receiving from the generations before us and passing on to the generations after us.

Back to the text: Our God also gave us a job. The need to work is part of the perfect creation of God. In all His creation, God hid many marvelous secrets. He told those in whom He had breathed the breath of life that they were to use the power He gave them to develop all nature. Notice how the two jobs fit together to become one. When we use all the things God put in His creation, we earn a living so we can give to our families or the people for whom we are responsible. When we need to take care of our families, we turn to the resources that God has provided for us to use.

At first it was a simple matter: for example, a farmer like Cain or a shepherd like Abel. Both worked with the tools God had provided. But soon the list of possible vocations increased. The third occupation mentioned in the Bible is musician, the next, those who work with metals.

As the number of people increased, so did the number of possible occupations. They had a need to eat, to have clothing, to have a home. Through their jobs God gave people what they needed. Every record of early human beings shows how all people have a need to create. They drew pictures in caves. They carved stones and built monuments. They sang and played music. They wrote a record of themselves. They discovered more and more of the secrets God had hidden in His creation.

Today, people work with neutrons, megabytes, DNA, and numerous other resources unknown only a few years ago. But nothing new has been created. We have found what God has created, and we are aware that the search goes on. We are doing the work God gave us.

The career you are preparing for, the job you have, or the occupation from which you have retired tie together the assignment given to you by your Creator. God has asked you to work with Him. Through your work you use His resources to provide for yourself and your family. Through your work you take your place in that long line of generations that have looked for and used the resources of God's creation.

What has God placed under your charge? Identify the part of His creation that is under your supervision. For the children: your toys, your room, your pets, your schoolwork, your clothes. For the retired: your investments, your home, your recreation. For the employed: your job description at work, your education, your abilities, your property, your assets. For all of us: our relationships in our families and our communities. These are the things in the garden that we are to tend.

Part 2

Text: Genesis 3:15–19

But that was a perfect world. Adam and Eve damaged the life of togetherness that God had given them when Eve gave Adam the forbidden fruit and he told on her to God. They failed at their job when they decided to run the Garden of Eden the way they wanted to rather than the way the Creator had told them to do it.

From our point of view outside the Garden, God had three choices.

- He could have destroyed the first couple, but He is a Creator, not a destroyer.

- He could have ignored their sin and let them continue to run things their way. Then they would have destroyed all that He had created, including themselves.

- He could have taken away their partnership with Him and forced them to do things His way. But He had breathed into them His own life. They could not become robots.

God found another way to deal with Adam and Eve's sin. He did not destroy them nor did He ignore their evil. Instead, He shackled them with the responsibility they made. He had given them responsibility and they had failed, so they also received the responsibility for their failure.

Listen to the text: First, their sin affected having children, their job of continuing the creation. There would be pain in childbirth. They were later to discover that those pains were only the beginning of the ache of being the parents of sinners like themselves. The pain of childbirth became the introduction to the pain of parenthood.

Next in the text, God tells them how their job would be affected by their sin. They would be overworked. There would be weeds in their fields and thorns in their orchards. They would have to eat things they didn't like. They would sweat as they worked. They were still God's partners, but they weren't in the garden God had first given them. They were in Eden East, a place where they still had the resources the Creator had given them but where they could do things their way rather than His way.

You and I also live in Eden East. We live in a world that God created but one we want to run by our rules. God has not fired us, but He lets us see what we have done to His creation.

How does our mutiny against our Creator affect your family relationships? How does the human rule—everyone-must-do-it-my-way—affect your family? How much pain have you caused your family because you insist that they do things your way? How much pain have others caused you because each believes in self-rule? The pain of childbirth was only the beginning.

Adam's job included weeds and thorns. What are the weeds and thorns in your job? How do you feel when you go to work? When you leave work to come home? Do you do your job because you want to or because you have to? Do you do your work only because you need the paycheck? Do you have a need to do something worthwhile? What satisfaction do you get from your work?

Our Creator has not given up on us. Inside each of us is an awareness that we were made for a reason. Each of us is still a clod off the block of soil from which Adam was formed. Each of us still has the breath of the Creator in us.

But our judgment about how we do our work has been affected by our rebellion against God. We want to do it our way. Our early ancestors who built the tower at Babel were not wrong in their desire to build. They could have built the tower to the glory of God, who had created them. It could have been a witness of their relationship to the Creator. Instead, they built it to their glory so we would remember them as important people.

We need to be productive, but what we produce never turns out as great as it seemed in our plans. Others do not recognize the greatness of what we do because each one is struggling with his or her own frustrated effort at being productive. We compete with one another because we have forgotten that we are all on the same team, serving the same Creator. We are in a catch-22. We need to achieve something because the breath of the creative God is in us. But what we do includes weeds and sweat because the DNA of our sinful ancestor Adam is also in us.

Part 3

Text: 1 Peter 4:10–11

God's way of helping us out of our catch-22 cost Him dearly. Because we are responsible for our actions, for the sin we commit, we suffer the consequences. But God sent His Son to live in Eden East with us. God became human in Jesus Christ. Jesus became one with us through the reproductive system God had created but without the transmission of human guilt. Jesus came to take a job on earth that included weeds and sweat. He came to earn a new listing for God in the Yellow Pages. He is there as the only entry under *Savior.* He took the consequences for our sin. He is the only one who has died for the sins of all and who won the victory for all over death by rising from the dead.

Jesus was God's partner in creation, and He became our partner as managers of God's creation here. The text tells us, "Each one, as a good manager of God's different gifts, must use for the good of others the special gift he has received from God" (1 Peter 4:10).

Because Jesus Christ has redeemed you, your relationship with your family and your occupation again becomes part of your relationship with your Creator. God has not given up on us. Even though we still are shackled with our sins and their results, God lets us serve Him. We can use our need to be productive as part of our partnership with God.

We are still in Eden East for a reason. We are not serving a sentence in exile because of our sins. Instead, we are agents of grace in a world of sin. As we live with the weeds and the sweat of our jobs, we are aware that we are in the arena of the war that God has declared to regain His creation from the power of the tempter. The weeds and the sweat are still there, but they give us a different message. No longer do they condemn us. Instead, they make us see the victory we will have when we are freed from the sin that will destroy this world. The weeds and sweat of our jobs give us a chance to use the grace that Jesus Christ gives us so we still may be workers in God's creation.

You came to church today to worship God. We have received His Word through Jesus that gives us both the message of forgiveness and the message of encouragement. We have received these gifts and strengthened one another. As you return to your place of work in your home and on your job, you continue worshiping God by using the special gift that God has placed in you to serve Him by serving others.

Children's Sermon

Text: Jonah 4:7

Concept: A Job You Can Do

In the story of Jonah, God asks for help three times. First, He asks

Jonah to be a prophet *(hold up prophet picture)* and deliver His message to Nineveh, a city across land to the east. Jonah didn't want to do the job, so he hopped on a boat going west.

But God still wanted Jonah to do the job. He asked for help a second time. Jonah was tossed into the sea, and God sent a big fish *(hold up fish picture)* to swallow him. In the fish's stomach, Jonah had no choice about which direction he would go. The fish took him east again, and spit him up on the beach.

Jonah decided he had better do what God had told him to do. He went to Nineveh and delivered God's message. The people believed him and repented. God forgave them. Jonah didn't want the Ninevites to be forgiven. He went outside the city and pouted under the shade of a tall plant.

God now asked for help a third time. He sent a worm *(hold up worm picture)* to chew on the plant that shaded Jonah. The plant died, and the shade was gone. Jonah had to learn the same lesson that the people of Nineveh learned. He needed to repent and ask God for forgiveness.

The big fish gets most of the attention in this story because it did such a special thing. Most people don't know about the worm because it just did what worms usually do—it chewed on a plant.

God also has asked all of us to work for Him. When we say we can't because we are sinners, God sends someone to tell us that Jesus is our Savior and we are forgiven so we can work for Him.

Some day each of you may be big fish and do great and wonderful things. But you don't have to wait until then to do what God asks you to do. The worm did what worms usually do, and that was exactly what God wanted. You can do what kids usually do. You can play and have fun. You can learn about the great world God has created. You can be part of a family. You can love and serve Jesus.

No one knew that the worm that lived at the time of Jonah would be recorded in history, but you and I talk about it today. You do not have to become a big fish and be famous. You can serve God because He made you and because Jesus is your Savior.

Prayers

Continue offering support to worshipers in their occupational needs:

- Include a different career field in the congregational prayers each week. Select a broad category (for example, educators, farmers, medical personnel, engineers, politicians, factory workers, homemakers, students, etc.) that may cover the types of employment in your congregation. List the prayers in the bulletin and church calendar. Accept requests for categories to be included.

- In the prayers, include members of the congregation who work in the fields you mention, those who are preparing to do such work, and others who do the work for the benefit of those who are in worship.

For the Bulletin

For Participation during the Sermon

Part 1: Genesis 1:26–30

Which relationships are an important part of your purpose in life? Which part of God's creation has been placed under your management?

Part 2: Genesis 3:15–19

What pains do you have because of family relationships? What are the "weeds and sweat" in your job?

Part 3: 1 Peter 4:10–11

What are you doing to help family members receive the blessings that God wants them to have? What does your job provide for others in your community? in your country? in the world?

Through the Week

In the play "Light at the Top of the Stairs," a woman plans a surprise trip for her husband, who is retiring from a lumberyard. He is not happy about the gift. She says, "Fun is going to Hawaii." He says, "No, fun is smelling sawdust."

1. What is fun for you?

2. What is fun in your family relationships?

3. Is it fun for you to do things so others in your family can have fun?

4. What do others in your family do to help you have fun?

5. What about your work is fun for you?

6. Are you willing to do the things at work that are not fun so you can have other results that are good for you and your family?

7. Can you do the things that you don't like to do without resenting them and causing them to ruin the good parts of your job?

8. Do you realize how many others are working to help you?

9. How many worked so that you could have breakfast this morning?

10. How many worked to make it possible for you to travel to work?

11. How many worked to help you enjoy your recreation/entertainment/vacation?

12. How many people help you in your spiritual life?

5

Divorce

Why So Sensitive?

Several generations ago most churches dealt with divorce by ignoring it. Those who were divorced were excommunicated—except for the "innocent party" in those rare cases when one partner committed adultery. Many unchurched people today still tell an angry story about how divorced parents or grandparents were treated by the church.

The rate of divorce has skyrocketed. The United States has the highest divorce rate in the world. Those nations that have outlawed all divorce (such as Brazil) have an even greater problem with children who have no legal identity because their parents are not married to each other. Very few families today are unaffected by divorce.

Most congregations now accept divorced and remarried members. That is progress for the church if it means that divorce is now treated like all other sins—that is, if the message of repentance and forgiveness is offered through Jesus Christ. However, it is not progress if it means that divorce is ignored or justified by legal and psychological arguments. Because we live in a sinful world, some divorces may be necessary. That does not mean that they are justified before God as right. We must move the reasons for divorce from the court of justice to the throne of grace.

It is difficult to preach about divorce because it means picking on one sin, and the preacher's goal is to help each worshiper see his or her sin. But marriage and divorce need to be addressed in sermons because they affect all people—even those who have never been married or divorced.

The suggestions offered in this sermon are about marriage and its place in the entire community. Unfortunately, we preachers do our best talking about marriage at weddings. Those who hear the sermons are guests rather than parishioners. The following sermon could be announced in the bulletin the week before the service as a wedding service to which all are invited as both guests and members of the wedding party.

Suggested extra resources for the one who prepares this sermon and as suggested reading for those who hear the sermon include: *I Take Out the Garbage Because I Love You* by this author and his wife, Carolyn Weisheit; *501 Practical Ways to Love Your Wife and Kids* by Roger Sonnenberg; *501 Practical Ways to Love Your Husband and Kids* by Jennifer Baker. All are available from Concordia Publishing House.

Prayer of the Day

Lord God, we ask You to be part of each of our human relationships, especially those of husband and wife, parents and children, and all our extended family members, through Jesus Christ our Lord. Amen.

Sermon

Text: Matthew 19:3–9
Concept: Members of the Wedding Party

Today's text, and therefore today's sermon, is about marriage—not just the individual marriage of one man and one woman but about marriage as part of the church and part of the community.

True, a marriage is the union of one man and one woman, but many more people are involved in a marriage. Think about the wedding ceremony. There is a bride and a groom, of course. But many others are involved in the wedding. *(Name attendants, family members, friends, musicians, caterers, photographers, etc.)* Even a simple wedding cannot be a private affair. Witnesses and an official are needed. And a wedding involves many people who may not attend the ceremony.

As we listen to Jesus, we want to see marriage and divorce from the view of one man and one woman united as one *and* as the involvement of many others. If you are married, this text applies to your marriage. If you have been married and are divorced, this text is for you. If your spouse has died, find comfort in this word from Jesus as you deal with your grief. If you will be married some time, let this story help you make those plans. If you haven't been married, and never will be, you also need the message Jesus has for you because you live in a world of married people. You are a member of the wedding.

I hope I have included all of you as you think about your past, present, or future marriages. Now think about how many other people are involved in your marriage—not just those who may have been in your wedding party, but those who are happy if your marriage is good for you, and those who would be hurt if you are hurt in your marriage relationship. Think of your family and friends who would cry with you if you lost your spouse through death or divorce. Think of those who rejoice with you at your anniversaries and other celebrations that are part of your marriage. To the singles: Think of the married people who provide companionship for you and care about you.

One more step: Think of how many other marriages affect you. You share the joys and sorrows of those whom you love. Marriage is the greatest source of both joy and sorrow.

No marriage is the property of only one man and one woman. We need community. Everything we do—the laws we have in our country, the circumstances of our employment, the activities at this church—involves the concept of marriage. Those who are not married, and never will be, are still part of many marriage relationships. You are blessed by the marriages of others. You are hurt by the marriages of others. Other people who are married need you as part of their spiritual, family, and personal life.

Marriage is a big deal—we're all in it together! Let's look at the text to see where you fit in the wedding party.

Application: (*Use in any order according to your congregation's needs. Add others according to local need.*)

1. You are a spouse. After all the discussion about divorce, Jesus leads the conversation back to creation when God established the marriage relationship. "They are no longer two, but one. Man must not separate, then, what God has joined together" (Matthew 19:6). God not only joins a husband and wife together, He also keeps them together. (*Discuss the need for repentance and forgiveness between husband and wife.*) Because you have stayed married does not mean that God loves you more than if you became divorced. Rather, your marriage is also under God's grace that we receive through Jesus Christ. Most people who get a divorce will recognize that, had they recognized their problems earlier and asked for help, the marriage could have been saved. Does your marriage need help? How can God help you maintain a good marriage?

   How can you help other people stay in a marriage? Do you have family or friends who are in a difficult marriage? They do not need you to tell them to get a divorce or not to get a divorce. They need you to love them, listen to them, and give them the love they need so they may love each other. Check the way you talk about your marriage or other marriages. Do you ridicule your husband or your wife? Do you degrade your marriage or the marriage of others?

2. You are divorced. Have you dealt with the issues that caused your divorce? Do you carry guilt because of your failure? Do you still blame the previous spouse and the previous in-laws? Divorce is sin because it divides what God brought together. You may feel that God did not bring you together, that the sin was the way you got married rather than the way you got divorced. That could be true. But in either case, you need to repent and ask God for forgiveness through our Savior.

   In our world today divorce is common. People have so many reasons for divorce: incompatibility, unfaithfulness, we-were-too-young-when-we-got-married, conflicts from family and job, and the list goes on. Each of these are real problems and cause pain and sorrow. Divorce may be necessary—but not on the basis of one spouse being right and the other wrong. Sin in a marriage is part of the property settlement. Do not try to give custody of the guilt to the other spouse and do not keep it for yourself. You have a Savior who died for your sins and for those of your spouse. Jesus takes custody of the sin and gives forgiveness. He frees you from the need to carry anger and the need for revenge against your ex. He frees you from the load of guilt that makes you afraid of future relationships.

Divorce cannot be placed in a separate category of sin. When Jesus says we cannot divorce one spouse and marry another, He is not refusing forgiveness for this sin. Instead, He makes it very clear that one does not divorce the present spouse because another one is waiting in the wings. The order is not married, divorced, remarried. The order is married, divorced, repentance and forgiveness, singleness, and then the start of a possible future relationship. Jesus is preventing divorced people from carrying problems from one marriage into another. The pain and guilt of the first marriage must be removed by Christ's suffering and death for us. Only then can another relationship be considered. Consider also whether a prospective spouse has dealt with previous relationships.

3. You are a widow or widower. You have had a marriage that ended with death. The commitment is gone, but the love isn't. You also need time to grieve for the spouse that you lost. Those who are widowed have a tendency to forget the problems in marriage—the kind that divorced people have to face. Your deceased spouse was not perfect, and neither were you. Let repentance and forgiveness (received and given) be part of your grief. Take the time to become single again. Do not try to replace the past relationship. You are a different person because of your first marriage. Consider also the effects of previous marriages or relationships that will affect a possible new spouse.

4. You are single in a world of married people. How you relate to those who are married depends on how you see your singleness. Are you glad that you are not married? Have you done yourself or someone else a favor by staying single? The Bible does not say that all people must be married. Jesus was single. But it does say that it is not good for you to live alone. That does not mean you must have a live-in in the present usage of the term. It does mean you need relationships with others, and they with you. Many of these relationships will involve married people, and you will become part of their marriage relationship. You need not be a fifth-wheel, unless you accept the role.

You are single and plan to get married. One of the great mysteries of human nature is the selection of a spouse. Some couples are very much alike: same faith; same background; same interests, goals, and values; even the same hobbies. Some with those qualities have great marriages; others end up divorced. Some couples are the opposite of each other, far beyond male and female. Some have none of the similarities mentioned above. Some have great marriages; some end up getting divorced.

You are responsible for the choice of your spouse. God even made Adam take the responsibility of making a choice among the creatures He had created that day. Marriages are not made in heaven—they are made on earth, for the earth. You have to first be a *one*—that is, to know who you are as an individual, mature and able to accept the responsibility of marriage. Then you can become one who becomes two and yet remains one.

Conclusion:

You need others as you make decisions regarding marriage—the decision to get married, the decision to stay married, and the decision to help others in their marriage. View yourself as part of a large wedding party. Jesus is also a member of that wedding party. When someone asks, "Who speaks the message of Christ's love and forgiveness to this husband and wife?" you get to answer, "I do."

Children's Sermon

Text: Matthew 19:3–9

Concept: Plan Your Marriage

(Prior to the service ask a couple to help. If possible ask a couple who soon will be married. Otherwise select a newly married couple or a couple celebrating a major anniversary. Adjust the message accordingly.)

(Talk about why the children come to the front of church during the children's sermon.) Do you know any other reasons why people come to the altar? *(Mention the Lord's Supper, baptism, etc.)* There's another reason people come to the front of church—weddings. *(Invite the couple to stand at the altar with the children around them.)*

Most of you will probably get married some day. *(Talk about what they need to do to plan a wedding, including planning for clothes, flowers, pictures, etc. Always mention that there is something more important.)*

Getting married in church does not require all those things that we often have at weddings. A church wedding means that Jesus is invited to be there. The husband and wife are asking Jesus to bless their marriage. Husbands and wives need to know they are forgiven by Jesus, and they need to know how to forgive their partner in Jesus' name.

Some people have wedding books that tell how to plan all the things that people like to do when they get married. *(Hold up a Bible.)* This book helps a man and woman plan more than just the wedding. It also helps them plan the marriage as a man and woman promised to be husband and wife.

For the Bulletin

If you are married, list others who are affected by the joys and sorrows of your marriage.

For everyone, list the marriages of others that affect your life.

If you plan to get married, think of people you know who have the kind of marriage you would like to have. Think of those who have the kind of marriage you would not like.

Through the Week

Make one list of items that help build up marriage and one list of items that degrade marriage. Watch in the following areas for examples: TV, newspapers and magazines, conversations at work and at home, and social activities.

Helping the Needy

Why So Sensitive?

The Gospel of Jesus Christ changes us. Our sinful nature makes us selfish. But Christ has taken care of us so we can take care of one another. The major theme of Scripture is that God loves us so we can love one another. Our faith in Christ will make us want to love and help others.

But what happens when it doesn't happen? Do those who say they love God but do not show love to others (or show selective love) deny their faith? John writes, "We love because God first loved us. If someone says he loves God, but hates his brother, he is a liar" (1 John 4:19–20). Strong language.

As you preach to a Christian congregation, you have a responsibility to help believers put their faith into action. However, your message must be the Gospel continued, not a return to the Law. A simple language lesson:

> You are saved by Jesus, but you must still do good works.
> You are saved by Jesus, and now you can do good works by His power.

Notice that the first sentence reverses field and goes back to the Law. The second assures the hearer of salvation through Christ and continues the Good News that Jesus is with us in our daily lives.

Sermons that ask Christians to put their faith into action can fall into a ditch on either side of the road. One ditch is the sermon that urges acts of Christian love and charity but does not tell the hearers how to do those things. The opposite ditch is to promote a program or agency as if it were the only way to live out the Christian life.

Christians need to have their faith challenged. Our faith is like our muscles and our mind—use it or lose it. When those who love Jesus also love those whom Jesus loves, their faith is in use.

Suggested Readings

Psalm: Psalm 146:5–7

First Lesson: 2 Kings 7:3–9

Second Lesson: Philippians 4:9–13

Gospel: Matthew 25:31–46

Prayer of the Day

We have come, Lord Jesus.
We are Your guests.
Through Your gifts to us,
May others be blessed. Amen.

In the following sermon suggestions, the children's message is first because it is often first in the worship service. In this case it is an introduction to the sermon. If you do not use a children's sermon, use the material from it as the introduction to the sermon proper. For both sermons you will need a large box labeled "Care Package from Heaven." The words should be large enough for people in the back row to read.

Either handwrite or computer generate pieces of paper with the message "Someone in heaven loves me!" in large type. You'll need one copy for each child who comes forward for the children's sermon—you also may want to give one to each adult.

Children's Sermon

Text: Philippians 4:9–13

Concept: Someone in Heaven Loves Me

(Before the children's sermon, place the papers with the message "Someone in heaven loves me!" in the large box. Make sure you have enough for every child to receive one at the appropriate time.) This box was delivered to the church. It has something for you. *(Talk about the message on the box. Explain words according to children's ages.)*

A care package is special because it is a message about love. Let me show you how it works. Suppose I know someone who is hungry and I have lots of food. I can put some food in the box and give it to the person who is hungry. *(Use other illustrations: Someone needs clothes. Someone needs toys.)*

Our Bible reading was written by Paul. He knew how to use a care package. He knew that Jesus had died to forgive all people and to take them to heaven. So he traveled to many places and told people that Jesus loved them. But some people didn't like what Paul did, so they put him in jail. Then the people who had learned about Jesus from Paul had a chance to give a care package to him. They brought food, clothing, and books to Paul to help him. They also could tell Paul that Jesus loved him, just as he had told them about Jesus.

Now I get to give you something from this box. *(Hand out the pieces of paper. Discuss who in heaven loves us. Ask how Jesus loves us. Suggest places to put the message about God's love.)* You received something from the care package from heaven. You also can use the care package to give your love to others. *(Talk about ways we can give to others. Mention concrete things like food, clothing, etc. but also talk about kindness, forgiveness, etc.)* You can use the care package from heaven two ways. First, it tells you how God cares for you and blesses you. Then you can use the package to care for others.

The Sermon

Text: Philippians 4:9–13

Concept: Care Package from Heaven

(Ask your hearers to identify what God has sent them. Use the box as a symbol of the work of the Holy Spirit, who brings us the gifts of God. Put items in the box: Bible, communion wafer, a baptismal certificate, a cross, a church directory [a symbol of Christian fellowship], food, medicine, clothing. You may want to ask worshipers for other suggestions.)

The care package from heaven offers all this to us. But the box always contains more than we need. We who receive from the box also get the box. We now can pass it to others.

Application: *(Use in any order according to your congregation's needs. Add others according to local need.)*

1. We use the care package from heaven in our congregation. People who receive the Gospel provide the Gospel for others. *(Mention activities in your congregation that offer blessings to members and also give members an opportunity to pass the box to others: worship, fellowship, education, caring ministries, social ministries.)*

2. We have received so much from God that we can offer the care package from heaven to the neighborhood. *(List things that your congregation does to bring God's blessings to others in the community. Suggest other things that could be done. Mention things done by individuals as well as those done by the congregation.)*

3. *(Suggest ways that your people can pass the box beyond your congregation and neighborhood.)* Because of worldwide communication, we know about the needs of people in many places. We have ways to reach out to those people. *(Mention specific programs offered by your denomination or by other international groups. Suggest how local people can participate.)*

4. You may want to provide a box (or envelope) labeled "Care Package from Heaven" for each worshiper to take home. This is especially helpful if you want to encourage believers to participate in a specific program. However, make the goal that each person helps others, and offer the program as one way to do so. Remind them of Paul's view that the people had always loved him but had not had an opportunity to show it. This program is one opportunity for your members to show their love.

5. Both in the collective ministry of the church and the individual ministry of each believer, we can see some needs very clearly. Hungry people need food. God has placed food in His care package to us. We can send the package to others. *(List other needs such as clothing, medical care, housing.)* But remember that healthy and wealthy people also need help. They need God's love through Jesus Christ. They need forgiveness. They need a way to serve God. Like the people in Paul's time, they need an opportunity to help others. We can provide that opportunity.

6. If your congregation has some special need to help others, make suggestions for continued use of the care package from heaven. Make it into a container for people to bring food for the community food bank. Place it on the altar for special offerings. Use the box to collect gifts for needy children. Invite the congregation to add to this list.

Conclusion:

God sends the box to you. Help yourself. Pass it on.

Congregational Participation

Perhaps your congregation already has a food barrel to collect groceries to be distributed through a local food bank or by your church. If not, this would be a good time to start. Some group might make a banner that could be displayed when there is a special need for food.

For the Bulletin

1. As you listen to the sermon, write down what God has sent to you in the care package from heaven.

2. Make a prayer list of what you want to ask God to send to you.

3. What has God given you in such abundance that you can fill another care package from heaven to pass on to others?

Take-Home Devotion Page

Monday

Read the sermon text (Philippians 4:9–13) again. What did the sermon give you? What did it ask you to do? How does verse 13 help you do it?

Tuesday

Read Matthew 25:31–46.

Wednesday

How have others loved you this week? Who has shown you the kindness that comes from Jesus?

Thursday

How have you loved others this week? To whom have you passed on the gifts that Jesus has given you?

Friday

Read 1 John 4:18–21.

Saturday

How has last weekend's worship helped you during this week? What help do you need as you prepare to worship again this weekend?

Choral Reading

In His Glory (A Choral Reading of Matthew 25:31–46 NIV)

Cast

Reader (standing at a podium in the center)

1, 2, 3, 4, and 5 (standing on the reader's right)

A, B, C, D, and E (standing to the reader's left)

A choir may be used, if necessary, to support the two brief singing sequences.

READER: The Bible reading for today is from Matthew's gospel, chapter 25, beginning at the 31st verse: "When the Son of Man comes in His glory …"

A: "In His glory?" What's that?

B: Sounds like a foreign car. Probably made in Greece.

C: I think it's one of those new airplanes—The Glory 657 or something like that.

D: No, it's a new kind of suit. I saw Michael Jackson in a glory suit the other night.

READER: When the Son of Man comes in His glory, and all the angels with Him …

2: Wow! He'll come with angels.

5: With all of His angels.

4: The event is so important that none of the angels will have to stay behind to tend the store.

3: And none of the angels will be on duty guarding our ways to keep us from striking our feet against a stone.

1: But we'll never get to see that kind of glory.

READER: When the Son of Man comes in His glory, and all the angels with Him, He will sit on His throne in heavenly glory.

E: Now He has a throne in heavenly glory.

A: I didn't think His glory was a car or an airplane.

D: Well, He can't travel around in a throne. Maybe His throne of heavenly glory came out of His glory car.

C: Maybe it came out of the Glory 657. I hear they're fancy.

B: Let's face it. We don't know what His glory is.

D: But we should find out. We might like some of His glory too.

E: And He might share it with us. He's nice that way.

READER: When the Son of Man comes in His glory, and all the angels with Him, He will sit on His throne of heavenly glory.

5: Imagine! A throne of heavenly glory!

3: I bet it's made of ivory and gold with diamonds all over.

2: No, I think it will be made of light and energy—so bright that we won't be able to look at it.

4: But we'll hear the music.

3: No, we'll never get that close to His glory.

1: Won't they have a P.A. system so everyone can hear?

5: I don't care if we get to see or hear it. I just want to know when it happens.

READER: All the nations will be gathered before Him.

C: All the nations?

A: I wonder if that means just the nations that exist today or all that have ever existed.

E: Well, I hope they don't put us next to the Arabs.

B: I don't want to be next to one of those tribes that goes naked.

C: We vacationed in Central America last summer. You should see some of the beautiful figurines I bought. But, frankly, those people don't smell good. I won't want to be near them.

D: Don't worry about it. I'm sure our nation will have a good spot. After all, He always takes good care of us.

READER: All the nations will be gathered before Him, and He will separate the people one from another as a shepherd separates the sheep from the goats.

4: How does a shepherd separate sheep from goats?

2: Maybe by their smell. I've heard that goats stink.

1: Anyone can tell a sheep from a goat. How He does it is not the problem.

4: Then the question is: Why? Why does the shepherd separate the goats from the sheep?

3: Because the goats serve one purpose and the sheep another.

5: If they were all the same, He wouldn't have to separate them.

1: Then will He separate us according to our purpose?

2: Or according to the way we have followed His purpose?

4: I'm afraid we don't know enough about shepherds.

3: Or maybe we don't know how to be sheep.

READER: Then the King will say to those on His right, "Come, you are blessed by My Father; take your inheritance, the kingdom prepared for you since the creation of the world."

2: Us? Do you mean us?

4: Come, with You? Forever?

5: A kingdom prepared for us!

1: Blessed by Your Father?

READER: Then He will say to those on His left, "Depart from Me, you who are cursed, into the eternal fire prepared for the devil and his angels."

C: Who do you think you're talking to?

D: There must be some mistake.

A: Eternal fire?

E: I appeal to a higher court.

B: But we've always called You our Lord.

READER *(to the right):* For I was hungry and you gave me something to eat.

3: Lord, when did we see You hungry and feed You?

READER *(to the left):* For I was hungry and you gave Me nothing to eat.

D: Lord, when did we see You hungry?

READER *(to the right):* I was thirsty and you gave Me something to drink.

2: When did I see You thirsty and give You something to drink?

READER *(to the left):* I was thirsty and you gave Me nothing to drink.

C: When did I see You thirsty and give You nothing to drink?

READER *(to the right):* I was a stranger and you invited Me in.

4: When did we see You a stranger and invite You in?

READER *(to the left):* I was a stranger and you did not invite Me in.

A: I never saw You as a stranger. I've always known You.

READER *(to the right):* I needed clothes and you clothed Me.

5: Lord, when did I clothe You?

READER *(to the left):* I needed clothes and you did not clothe Me.

B: I never saw You without clothes. I don't go around looking at naked people.

READER *(to the right):* I was sick and you looked after Me.

1: When did I see You sick, Lord?

READER *(to the left):* I was sick and … you did not look after Me.

E: I'm sure You've never been seriously ill, Lord. I mean, with Your miracles and everything. But if You were, I'm sorry. If I had known about it, I'd have sent You a card.

READER *(to the right):* I was in prison and you came to visit Me.

4: I have visited prisons, Lord, but I didn't know You were there.

READER *(to the left):* I was … in prison and you did not look after Me.

D: Well, You can hardly expect everyone to visit a prison. And You were jailed such a short time. Only overnight, if I remember correctly. Besides, I wasn't living then.

E: There must be some mistake. You've known us for a long time.

C: We've always gone to church.

A: And served on committees.

B: And attended conventions.

C: We've done the things we thought were important.

D: Remember the beautiful banners we made to praise You?

E: Remember how often we sang our praise to You?

B: One of the songs is about Your glory. We do know about Your glory. Come on. Let's sing it.

A, B, C, D, E *(perhaps with a choir):*

> Glory be to God on high:
> And on earth peace, good will toward men.
> We praise You,
> We bless You,
> We worship You,
> We glorify You
> We give You thanks for Your great glory. (*Lutheran Worship*, p. 138)

READER *(to the left):* I was hungry and you gave Me nothing to eat, I was thirsty and you gave Me nothing to drink, I was a stranger and you did not invite Me in, I needed clothes and you did not clothe Me, I was sick and in prison and you did not look after Me.

A, B, C, D, E: Lord, when did we see You hungry or thirsty or a stranger or needing clothes or sick or in prison, and did not help You?

READER *(to the left):* I tell you the truth, whatever you did not do for one of the least of these, you did not do for Me.

B: The least?

C: The least of all of these?

D: Of all nations?

C: The people we didn't even know?

A: We would have helped You, Lord, but these …

E: Not just anyone who comes along.

D: Some people just don't want help. How are we to know whom we are to help?

READER: Then they will go away to eternal punishment. (*A, B, C, D, E leave*)

READER *(to the right):* Come, you who are blessed by My Father; take your inheritance, the kingdom prepared for you since the creation of the world.

2: Why us, Lord?

5: We did not recognize Your glory.

4: We do not deserve Your reward.

1: We don't want hell, but we don't deserve heaven.

READER: I was hungry and you gave Me something to eat, I was thirsty and you gave Me something to drink, I was a stranger and you invited

Me in, I needed clothes and you clothed Me, I was sick and you looked after me, I was in prison and you came to visit Me.

1, 2, 3, 4, 5: Lord, when did we see You hungry and feed You, or thirsty and give You something to drink? When did we see You a stranger and invite You in, or needing clothes and clothe You? When did we see you sick or in prison and go to visit You?

READER: I tell you the truth, whatever you did for one of the least of these brothers of Mine, you did for Me.

1: You mean You were there when we visited the nursing home?

5: You were there when we sent clothing to India?

3: We prayed in Your name when we visited in prison, but I never realized …

4: You were with me when I read to Mrs. Ellis.

2: You know about the food for the Dunman family.

READER: I tell you the truth, whatever you did for one of the least of these brothers of Mine, you did for Me.

1, 2, 3, 4, 5 (*perhaps with a choir*):

Glory be to God on high:
    And on earth peace, good will toward men.
    We feed You,
    We clothe You,
    We invite You,
    We look after You,
    We give You thanks for Your great glory.

1: That is His glory.

5: Not gold and ivory, but food for the hungry, water for the thirsty.

3: Not diamonds, but clothing for the poor.

4: Not light and energy, but company for the lonely.

2: Not special effects, but special services.

READER: And all the angels with Him and He will sit on His throne in heavenly glory.

4: He shares in our lives.

3: His glory is that He gave His life for us.

READER: All the nations will be gathered before Him, and He will separate the people one from another as a shepherd separates the sheep from the goats.

4: He gave glory to us when He loved us.

5: And we share His glory with others.

1: We have lived in His glory and didn't know it.

3: We have loved because He first loved us.

READER: Come, you who are blessed by My Father; take Your inheritance, the kingdom prepared for You since the creation of the world.

7

Grief

Why So Sensitive?

Grief is a sensitive subject—but not for the same reasons as most of the other sermon topics in this book. This is not a political issue. Grief is not the subject of debate in public arenas. Church denominations and political parties do not have opposing opinions.

Grief is sensitive because it is personal and private. In this worship service the goal will not be to move the subject from the court of justice to the throne of grace. Rather, it will be to move it from the counselor's couch to the throne of grace. Many people have not learned how to grieve because they grew up in families and in a society where grief was hidden and expected to be hidden. Some are ashamed of their grief because they think it is a weakness.

Most pastors give their best help to those who grieve in funeral sermons. That is good, but the depth of grief makes it difficult for mourners to benefit from the comfort that is given. Also most people at church funerals are not members of the congregation. The ideas for this worship service are offered to help the members of a congregation learn to deal with grief for themselves and to be of help to others.

Suggested Readings

Psalm: Psalm: 42:9–11

Old Testament: Deuteronomy 14:1–2 and/or 2 Samuel 12:16–23

Epistle Lesson: 1 Thessalonians 4:13–18

Gospel: John 11:33–37

Prayer of the Day

Holy Spirit, when our hearts are filled with grief, send others to comfort us with the love and presence of Jesus Christ. And send us with that same message to others whose hearts are full of grief. Amen.

Sermon

Text: 1 Thessalonians 4:13–18

Concept: The Ingredients of Grief

(Show a large jug with a label that says GRIEF *in large letters with smaller print beneath it.)* Today's sermon is about grief. I'd like you to see grief as a product in this jug. It is on the shelf at the supermarket. Grief is a product that we all need at special times. We also need to be aware of those special times when others need grief.

The greatest need for grief is at the time of death. You still may need to deal with grief for a death that occurred long ago. You, or someone you know, may be in need of grieving now because someone dear to you has died recently. In the future all of us will need to use this product. Our text tells us, "We want you to know the truth about those who have died." We need to know about death so we can deal with our grief and know how to help others in their grief.

Grief is needed at the time of a loved one's death. But it is not just the death of a person that causes grief. It may be the death of a marriage or other family or personal relationships. It may be the death of a dream, the loss of an ability, the disappointment of a failure.

The idea of this sermon is to "know the truth about those who have died." We do not hide the jug called grief. We do not use it alone in the darkness of night. We recognize that grief is a common human condition. The more we learn to share our grief with others and let others share their grief with us, the more we will see grief as a blessing that comes from love rather than a curse that comes from loss. It is because we love others and others love us that we feel the pain of grief. To avoid the possibility of grief in the future, we would have to avoid relationships of love. There is a better way.

We are going to look at grief not as a lone emotion, but as a part of our entire life. Those who are grieving also have other things happening in their lives. Those others things either add to the grief and make it more difficult or they ease the grief and help people survive their sorrow. Any product that you buy has a name that identifies it, just as this jug is labeled *GRIEF.* Products also have a list of ingredients. Grief can have different ingredients. Let's look at other emotions that are added to grief.

Application: *(Use in any order according to your congregation's needs. Add others according to local need.)*

1. When people feel grief, they often show it through other emotions that make the grief last longer, go deeper, and avoid the real issue of sorrow. These other emotions include:

- *Anger at others.* When anger is added to grief, the grief goes underground and remains untreated. *(Discuss how many people show grief (or avoid grief) by being angry at other family members, the hospital or doctors, the pastor or church members, etc.)*

- *Anger at the person.* An even more difficult form of anger added to grief is anger directed at the person who died. Often there are unresolved issues, a feeling of abandonment, or a failure to be honest about death that causes mourners to experience the conflict of sorrow about the death and at the same time anger at the person. We need to be free to admit the anger rather than bottle it up.

- *Guilt.* After a death, people ask, "What should I have done?" Sometimes loved ones feel they have failed the person who died. They didn't offer help. They didn't ask forgiveness for a certain problem. The death of a person is the end of a chapter for the one who died, but it is often the middle of a chapter for the ones who are left.

- *Loneliness.* Sometimes the person who died was ill for a long time and received constant care from a family member. That caregiver's purpose in life was to help the ill person. At death the caregiver loses not only the loved one but virtually his or her occupation.

- *Dealing with other struggles that are added to the pain of grief.* See each of them as an ingredient that affects the taste of grief.

2. The text offers other ingredients that can be added to grief.

- *Hope.* Note that the text does not tell us not to grieve, rather not to grieve as those who have no hope. Add hope to the jug of grief. Hope takes the bitterness out of grief. We do not take grief away from one another. Rather we bless it with the hope that we have in Jesus Christ. The grief we feel is for our loss now. The hope that we feel is for the loved one who died in Christ and for ourselves as we look to the reunion promised in verses 15–17 of the text.

- *Faith.* The source of that hope is faith. "We believe that Jesus died and rose again, and so we believe that God will take back with Jesus those who have died believing in Him." Our faith is not in ourselves nor is it in the goodness of the one who has died. Rather our faith is in Christ who has taken the responsibility of being the Savior for the one who died—and for us.

- *Encouragement.* We encourage one another with the words of this text. Because Christ has died in our place, we are not afraid of death. Death is not the future enemy that we must face but the past enemy that was defeated by Christ's death and resurrection. We accept our grief and the grief of others, but we also accept the encouragement that the Holy Spirit gives us through Jesus Christ.

- *Add other ingredients to the jug of grief, according to special needs.* In some cases you might add humor and forgiveness (that we forgive the wrongs that the deceased has done to us—especially necessary when there were strained family relationships) and others.

Conclusion:
    As you look at your jug of grief, do not try to deny those things that add

even more to the sorrow that you feel. Hiding those problems only makes them grow. Instead, look for the ingredients that Jesus has added to grief. He felt grief at the death of His friend Lazarus, as we will feel grief at the death of our loved ones. Jesus did something about it. He raised Lazarus from the dead. Then Jesus Himself died and rose again. So when we die, we also will be raised from the dead. So then, encourage one another with these words.

Children's Sermon

Text: Romans 6:4

Concept: Know What Death Is

One day Chris' teacher gave her a note to take home to her mother. The envelope *(hold up envelope)* was sealed. Chris wondered what was in the envelope. Was it homework? She wanted to play with a new game she had gotten for her birthday, and she didn't want to do homework. Did her teacher write a note to her mother to tell about the problem Chris had in the lunch room? It wasn't a big problem, but she knew her mother would be upset.

When Chris got home, she didn't give the note to her mother. She hid it in her room. But she couldn't enjoy her game because she kept thinking about the note. She didn't feel like eating dinner because she was worried. Finally, she gave the note to her mother. *(Open envelope.)* It is an invitation for Chris and her mother to go to a party at the school library. Chris was worried for nothing. She enjoyed her dinner and then went back to playing the game.

Some people worry about death just like Chris worried about that note. *(Hold up sealed envelope marked DEATH.)* The word death scares some people. What if they have an accident or get sick and die? What if Mom or Dad dies? Or maybe a good friend might get killed in a car wreck? Some people don't talk about death, but they worry about it. They hide it like Chris hid the envelope.

Instead of being afraid of death and hiding from it, let's open it up and see what it is. *(Open envelope and read Romans 6:4.)* God's Word tells us that we do not have to be afraid of death. God does not want us to die. It is our sin that makes us die, but Jesus already has died for us. He already has paid for our sin. God's Word says that when you were baptized you were connected to Christ. Because we are connected to Christ, He took our sins. After He died, He rose from the dead. Because we are connected to Christ, we can die and we will be raised from the dead.

It is good to know about death so you don't have to hide from it and be afraid. You may live a long time on this earth. I hope that you will have a healthy and happy life. Some day all of us will die, but we don't have to worry about that. We don't have to be scared. Jesus is with us now. He will be with us as long as we live here. Then He will take us to heaven and we will be with Him forever.

Death will not destroy us. It will be the invitation that Jesus gives us to be with Him in heaven.

Congregational Participation

As part of this service, the following suggestion could be included in the sermon or as a bulletin notice.

> Would you, or a group of you, like to help members of our congregation at their time of grief? One way to help would be to make a banner for use at funerals and for Sundays after a death in our congregation. Contact the church office for suggestions and patterns.

For the Bulletin

What caused the greatest moments of grief in your life? What other issues made the grief even more difficult? What helped you resolve the grief? Do you still need help dealing with grief? Whom can you ask for help?

Through the Week

Visit a cemetery. If you are too busy for such a trip, read the obituary page of your local paper. Think of those people who have died. What would you do to help those who mourn their deaths? Do you know someone who has lost a loved one recently? What could you do to help that person? Do you know what your loved ones believe so you can have hope at the time of their death? Do your loved ones know of your faith so they will have hope when you die?

Sanctity of Life

Why So Sensitive?

Many of the most politically divisive and personally painful subjects in our society come under the category of "sanctity of life." Consider

- abortion;
- assisted suicide;
- euthanasia;
- capital punishment;
- gun control; and
- control/legalization of drugs, tobacco, and alcohol.

Under the heading of crime, all these are big political issues. Under the heading of sin, all are big moral issues. Christians line up on both sides of each topic as they render to Caesar and go to the polls. But how do Christians deal with these issues when they are rendering to God?

Very often some parts of the church have entered the political fray to use the power of government to enforce their spiritual convictions on these issues. Equally often Christians have objected to the church becoming involved in political issues. While Christians of good will have different views on what to do about the issues that involve sanctity of life, the greater concern is how they use their faith in Jesus Christ to influence the world on such issues. God works through governments to punish those who do wrong and to reward those who do right (Romans 13:1–12). However, under the Gospel, Christians have a much higher morality and have the power of Christ to both forgive and change the sinner.

Too often the debate seems to be about right and wrong, with the conclusion that passing laws will fulfill a duty. In reality neither the laws of God nor the laws of state have achieved a high level of morality. The laws of state often seem to be at the lowest possible level for people to live together in reasonable safety. The Law of God holds us to a level far higher than any individual, let alone society, could reach. First, He said that we had to be even more moral than the teachers of the Law and the Pharisees (Matthew 5:20). Then He upped the requirement by saying, "You must be perfect—just as your Father in heaven is perfect" (Matthew 5:48).

No one will ever achieve such perfection under the Law. Jesus, who demanded perfection, also gives it to us by His suffering and death in our place. As Christians, we have a unique position on sanctity of life issues. As followers of Jesus, we are not sent to condemn the world but to tell the message that He has saved it (John 3:17). If we enter the debate on contemporary issues assuming the choice is condemning or condoning abortion, suicide, euthanasia, etc., we are losing the great message that God has given to us, first for our own good and then for the good of the world.

The following sermon is offered as both a message for a special sermon and as a model for dealing with sanctity of life issues as they regularly appear in scriptural texts.

Suggested Readings

Psalm: Psalm 8:3–9
First Lesson: Genesis 2:7, 21–23
Second Lesson: Romans 12:1–2
Gospel: Matthew 5:21–24

Prayer of the Day

Father, who has created all human life in Your image; Jesus, who came to save all human life by paying for our sin; Holy Spirit, who gives us the new life that will last forever, bless our lives and those who protect our right to live. Give us Your love so we may love all whom You have created, redeemed, and called to faith. Amen.

Sermon

Text: Genesis 2:7, 21–23

Concept: We're All in This Life Together

When God created human life, He took a glob of soil and formed the prototype for all human beings. (*Show a wadded up, empty balloon—one of the long tube kind used by those who make balloon figures.*) Like this, it had no shape. The greatness of God's creation is seen not only in the design of the human body but much more in the life that He placed in that body. The text says, "He breathed life-giving breath into his [the human's] nostrils and the man began to live." (*Blow up the balloon. Tie the end of the balloon. Suggestion for smokers and other oxygen-challenged preachers: Inflate the balloon several times before using it in the sermon.*)

The first human being was made from the soil of the earth and given life by the breath of God. God never again has taken soil to form a person. Never again has He created life by breathing His breath into a human form. When He made the second person, He took part of the first and made two lives that were still one. (*Twist the balloon near the middle so it has two sections.*)

To those two He gave the privilege and the responsibility of continuing His creation. Without going back to the soil, and without a new breath from God, Adam and Eve continued the act of creation. *(Again, twist the balloon several times to form small sections.)* By birth more human beings came into existence, but they were one human family.

So it has continued for countless generations. No new soil. No new breath. But many new people. Ideally, the many still remain one—one holy family because in each is the breath of the holy God who created them.

Realistically, we have divided that which God created to be one. In my balloon example, the separate people remain united. In real life, sin has come to divide us—nation against nation, race against race, community against community, family member against family member. If I snipped the sections of this balloon apart, the balloon would burst and be destroyed. That is what God meant when He told us that if we sin we will die.

But God wants us neither to die nor to be divided, so He sent His Son, Jesus the Christ, to become part of the soil of the earth and the breath of God that is human nature. *(Make one more twist in the balloon to form a section at one end.)* God became human in Jesus Christ so He could bring together the separated humanity that His creation had become.

We talk about the sanctity of life today. That is not a political description of humanity. It is a recognition that all people are part of the one creation of God. All of us today are part of the continuing creation that started with the lump of clay and the breath of God. Our life and the lives of all people have sanctity, that is, life is holy because God created it. Though our sin will burst the balloon and destroy life, God's holiness is still part of us in our sinfulness (James 3:9; 2 Corinthians 3:18). All God's creation lives in the struggle between the sin of our remodeled human nature and the Spirit that God breathed into us at creation and continues to renew by the power of Jesus Christ.

Application: *(Use in any order according to your congregation's needs. Add others according to local need.)*

1. Abortion is a moral issue. One of these sections of the balloon is the life of an unborn child. It is part of the one creation of God. Another section is the mother who might abort the child. Another is the medical person who might perform that abortion. The sanctity of life applies to all people. We cannot offer selective love to part of God's creation. God's creative power made us all. Christ's redemptive act saves us all. We can love the unborn child best by loving the mother who carries the child. We can love the mother by loving those who provide medical care and advice.

    The Law of God and the law of nations draw a line to show morality. God's line is much higher—He requires perfection. The lines drawn by government are much lower. People have to make decisions. A woman facing a multiple birth may be told that one or more of the fetuses must be aborted to save the life of the others. Siamese twins are born. Both will die unless they are separated. When separated, only one will die. In such decisions we do not go before God with the assurance that we know the right answer. We turn from the court of justice to the throne of grace.

2. Euthanasia, assisted suicide, and living wills are a big moral issue faced by many people. How do we portray the sanctity of life to those who are suffering and headed nowhere but death? In times past people died because no medical help was available. We praise God for the medical care that prolongs life, but is there a time when we need not prolong suffering? At one time pneumonia was called "the old person's friend" because it was a way people could die naturally. But now we can cure pneumonia.

Think of the difference between *allowing* a person to die and *causing* a person to die. Who dares to make such decisions? Can it be made by the medical profession or by lawmakers? Can it be made by family members who bear the burden of caring for an ill person—and the possibility of an inheritance at the time of death? Sin becomes part of everything. We do not help one another by judging and condemning. We need to be supportive and understanding. Our message is that we can help sinners. Our lives are connected by the God who created us and by the Savior who redeemed us.

3. Capital punishment, gun control, and legislation of drugs, alcohol, and cigarettes are all sanctity of life issues. The laws of government and the court of public opinion keep moving the line between right and wrong on such issues. But morality is not established by laws of government and public opinion. Something does not become right because a group of people say it is right. Something is not wrong because a group of people say it is wrong. By demanding our freedoms, we may cause the death of others. Laws have never and will never solve the problems on such issues.

Christians have a different approach. We know that we have fierce desires in us, but we also know that God's grace is greater (James 4:5–6). We do more to help show the sanctity of life when we treat all people as God's people. We have love for the victim and for the perpetrator. We have something greater to offer than the judgment of what is right and what is wrong. We can offer the forgiveness of Jesus Christ. The world can argue about what is right and wrong. We know Christ who helps even when we are wrong.

Conclusion:

Hours before His death on the cross, Jesus said, "I pray that they may all be one" (John 17:21). Jesus did not solve the problem of sin by destroying the humanity that God had created. He did not, and we cannot, cut off the worst sinners from the human race. If I cut one section out of this balloon, all sections are destroyed. Jesus found another way. He took the death that should have been ours *(Carefully untwist all the sections so the balloon becomes one again.)*

This sermon did not answer all the questions about sanctity of life that you and I face every day. But the Gospel of Christ does tell us that we need not depend on our righteousness. Frankly, many times we do not know what is right. We have been wrong in the past about what is right and what is wrong. We may be wrong again (John 16:8–11). But Christ is right. Our great message to the world is not our conclusions on moral issues. Our message is that Christ has forgiven us for our wrongs. We depend on His being right. Therefore, we accept others not on the basis that they are right or wrong but because Jesus Christ also offers them His rightness.

Children's Sermon

Text: Exodus 20:12

Concept: Who Made You?

(Hold up a cookie.) Who made this cookie? *(Identify who baked it. Then identify who produced the ingredients. Trace the ingredients back to God's creation. Do the same with an article of children's clothing.)*

Who made you? *(Let children respond.)* That's right, God did. He did it through parents. *(Read Exodus 20:12.)* This is a commandment. It also tells us how God works to keep creating people. God creates us by giving love to a man and a woman. God wants every child be born to a man and a woman who love each other. First, they learn to love each other, then their love produces another person. The love of a husband and wife makes them become a father and a mother.

Because of sin, things sometimes don't work the way God wants. Some children get to live with both their father and mother. Some have another man or woman who loves them like a father or mother.

God's commandment also tells us something else. When we learn to love from our parents, we grow up to love another person too. This message from God not only tells you to love your mother and father, it also reminds you how important it is for you to learn how to love so you can become a parent.

We know that God has given us our sexuality that leads to loving another person. That's how God created you through your mother and father, and that's how you can become a father or a mother. It is a special gift from God to love another person and to help create a baby.

Sometimes we don't understand our sexuality and we use it the wrong way. That's why God sent Jesus to help us. If we use sex without love, we hurt ourselves and someone else. We also may hurt the baby we helped make. Jesus forgives us if we do wrong, and He helps us do right. Jesus loves you so you can love Him. That also helps us love another person.

Now you have to learn how to be a kid. Enjoy being a child and learn how to grow up so you can become a man or woman who can love another person and have children that are loved too.

For the Bulletin

1. List the people who are important to you. How are these people connected to you?

2. List the people from whom you feel separated. What is it that divides you from them?

3. How can you increase the unity that you have with those you named in the first question?

4. How can you have a reunion with those whom you named in the second question?

Through the Week

1. Watch for discussions about sanctity of life issues. Do the conversations help bring people together or do they divide people?

2. Look for opportunities to help others see the sanctity of their lives.

3. When you talk about sensitive issues such as abortion, suicide, homosexuality, and other moral issues, remember that someone hearing you may have personal experience with such an issue or have family members involved with decisions regarding the issue. Can you say something that will help them receive the love that Christ gives to them?

Stewardship

Why So Sensitive?

Stewardship is a sensitive subject because it is about money. No matter how many times the stewardship committee and the pastor say it is about talents, time, and treasures, stewardship is about money. That is not bad. Look at it as a formula: talents × time = money. You use your abilities to work eight hours each day and you get paid for it.

But the equation goes back much further than an hourly wage. Study Deuteronomy 14:22–29. The people were to bring their produce (the results of their time and talent) to the place of worship. If that place was too far to carry the produce, they were to sell what they had raised on the farm, carry the money to the place of worship, and buy what someone else had produced to use for their offering. We follow the same process every Sunday when we convert our time spent using our abilities into cash or a check and put it in our offering envelope.

Talking about money is a sensitive subject because each person must make a decision about spending money. Those decisions show priorities. That is sensitive because many people do not want to admit their priorities, let alone expose them to others. Also, since the church establishes its priorities by how it asks for and uses money, many people see the stewardship program of a congregation as one more bid for a slice of their financial pie.

A stewardship sermon must move the subject of money from the financial page to the throne of grace. Biblical stewardship is about money, but it is not just about the money given to the church. People need spiritual help in the management of their money—all of it. They practice good stewardship when they buy their food and pay for their housing and all the other needs that are part of their lives.

Suggested Readings

The readings are part of the Bible study. If you choose to change the format from a Bible study to a sermon, select readings from those suggested in the study.

Prayer of the Day

Lord, bless the abilities, the time, and the money that You have given to us so we may use them to the glory of God, Father, Son, and Holy Spirit. Amen.

Sermon

The material offered here for a stewardship Sunday may be used in several ways.

1. Announce this service as a special event in the life of the congregation. Start the worship with the invocation and a hymn, then use the material as a Bible study presented to the entire congregation. Conclude with the prayers of the congregation, a hymn, and the benediction.

   If you use this idea, print the material for all worshipers. Provide Bibles in the pews. You will be able to have everyone look up all the Bible references, but select key verses for everyone to read. The leader may read or summarize the other portions. You also could assign certain verses ahead of time to individuals so they can read them without delay.

   In the introduction, welcome visitors and give two reasons why you are glad they are there. Clarify that the purpose of this worship service is not just for the financial program of your congregation but to recognize the need for all who are under the Gospel to work together as Christians. This worship service will help visitors at their home congregation too. If visitors are not members of a congregation, invite them to become part of your church. This worship service will help them see their need to be part of God's work. Your church can help visitors by sharing the Gospel with them and by giving them a place where they can share it with others.

2. The material may be divided into two or three sermons in regular worship services. If you do this, be aware that all people who attend the first may not be at the last and those at the last may not have been at the first. Make sure the Gospel is clearly presented in each sermon.

3. In some cases this material may be used as a Bible study in special stewardship meetings. Again, make copies for all who participate and (perhaps) send, or deliver, copies of the study to members who could not, or did not, attend.

The Need to Give

The first idea of an offering to God was not a sacrifice but a gift.

1. The Old Testament mentions many gifts or freewill offerings.

- Cain and Able felt a need to give a present to God (Genesis 4).

- Leviticus lists many freewill offerings (22:18, 21, 23).

- Ezra lists required sacrifices and freewill offerings (1:4).

- Psalm 119:108 says our thanks are a freewill offering.

2. The New Testament also speaks of giving our gifts to God.

- Jesus refers to gifts in Matthew 5:23f and Luke 21:1 (the "gift" is identified as money).

- Hebrews 5:1 says the priests gave sacrifices and gifts (repeated three times).

- Revelation 11:10: "They will celebrate and send presents to each other ..."

3. Do you feel a need to give?

- How can you give a gift to someone who has everything?

- Have you received a gift of little financial value that means a lot to you?

- Would that same gift have made you happy if it were given by another person?

- To whom do you feel a need to give gifts?

- Why do you want to give a gift to Jesus?

The desire to give to God is itself a gift from God. Our best gift is the love that makes us give.

Sacrifices are gifts designated for a special purpose.

1. Fellowship (peace, well-being) offerings (Leviticus 3). Example: Deuteronomy 14:22–29.

2. Repayment offerings (Leviticus 5:14f; 7:1ff. Note the 20 percent surcharge).

3. Sin offerings of many kinds and many places. Look specifically at the Day of Atonement (Leviticus 16).

4. Thank offering, used animal and grain sacrifices, also singing. (Hebrew: confession, thanksgiving, choir).

5. Designated offerings do not pay for services or blessings (see Acts 8:18–23).

6. Our worship (like that in the Old Testament) is centered around sacrifice.

- Christ has come as the Lamb of God.

- We give thanks as we receive the Lord's Supper.

- We give sacrifices of service, fellowship, thanksgiving, witness, commitment.

The Gift That Is Needed

The Old Testament way of giving.

1. People gave freewill offerings to build a place of worship (Exodus 25:1–9).

2. They also were charged a tax (Exodus 30:11–16).

3. They brought offerings for special items of worship (Exodus 35:20–29).

4. They used their abilities to build the place of worship (Exodus 35:30ff).

5. They were asked to give a tithe—10 percent of their income (Deuteronomy 14:22).

The New Testament way of giving.

1. The first Christians established a communal system (Acts 4:32–37). We still operate with a communal spiritual-care system. Could our medical-care systems, utilities, etc. operate so anyone could use the services and give what they want? We give not just to cover our spiritual needs but also for the needs of others.

2. They called people to work on their behalf—missions (Acts 6:1–7; 13:1–3).

3. They collected funds to help others—social ministry (Acts 11:27–30).

4. Paul's stewardship manual (2 Corinthians 8:1–9:15)

- It is for people who want to give (2 Corinthians 8:2–5).

- It was a self-administered test of love (2 Corinthians 8:1, 9).

- Offerings are to create unity, not division (2 Corinthians 8:20).

- Each one must make a commitment (2 Corinthians 9:7–9).

The Gift Needed in Our Congregation

Our budget for this year is _____.

Our income this year has been _____.

Our expenses this year have been _____.

Special reasons why our income was high or low:

Special reasons why our expenses were high or low:

If we had an increase in giving, we would do the following to increase ministry in our congregation:

If our offerings do not reach the amount planned, we will have to cut the following:

We ask each member to consider one of the following options:

(In this section provide a locally prepared form for each member or family. On it offer the options of a pledge, increased pledge, special one-time offering, several special offerings, or other needs established by local needs and opportunities.)

For the Bulletin

Please take this Bible study home with you to use for your family devotion. We did not have the time to look up each of the Bible references. Please read each suggested Bible verse by yourself or with your family.

Children's Sermon

Text: Luke 21:1–4

Concept: The Way Jesus Counts Money

(If your congregation regularly includes a children's sermon, it would be a good idea to include the children in this Bible study. Invite the children forward when Luke 21:1–4 is used.)

(Show the children an offering plate that contains a quarter and an offering envelope that says "$200" on it.) Which offering is more? *(Let children respond.)* Of course, the $200 is more when we take it to the bank. But this is a church. We put our offerings on the altar because they are gifts from God.

(Discuss Luke 21:1–4.) Why did Jesus say that the widow who gave two pennies made a bigger offering than those who gave a lot more money? Maybe this quarter was given by a child. In God's eyes that could be as much as a check for a lot more money.

We do not give money to the church to pay Jesus. Jesus loved us and gave us a lot more than money. He gave us Himself. Now He lets us work with Him. One way that we work together is by giving money so we can do all the things that help other people learn about Jesus. *(Name some things that the offerings fund.)* Our offerings help us share Jesus' love with everyone.